Contents

Any words appearing in the text in bold, **like this**, are explained in the glossary.

Introducing ingredients

Food groups

Classifications are often used to make things easier to understand. Food can be classified (grouped) according to a system of healthy eating. For example, the Food Standards Agency have developed the 'eatwell plate', which shows the types and proportions of foods we need to eat to have a healthy, well balanced diet.

The eatwell plate is based on the following five food groups:

- Bread, rice, potatoes, pasta and other starchy foods
- Fruit and vegetables
- Milk and dairy foods
- Meat, fish, eggs, beans and other non-dairy sources of protein
- Foods and drinks high in fat and/or sugar.

Nutrients

Dividing foods according to their main nutrient is a useful tool for anyone working with food. A **dietitian** needs a detailed knowledge of the nutrients contained within foods in order to advise clients or patients on the most suitable diet to follow. A **food technologist** needs to have a detailed knowledge of the physical properties of a food (as well as its nutritional content) in order to create a recipe that will be successful in large-scale production as well as in the test kitchen.

 In the eatwell plate, each food group is highlighted with a different colour. This helps us to see how much of what we eat should come from each group. Everything you eat is included, even snacks.

People who create menus or new food products need to understand dietary reference values (DRVs). These are quantities of different nutrients required daily by different groups of people. The calculations were first made by the Committee on Medical Aspects of Food Policy (COMA) for the UK in 1991. The measurements include:

- the lower reference nutrient intake (LRNI)
- the estimated average requirement (EAR)
- the reference nutrient intake (RNI).

RNIs are used for protein, vitamins and minerals and are an estimate of the amount that should meet the needs of a certain group of people, for example, females aged 11–14 years or males over the age of 65. The EAR is an estimate of the average amount of energy or a nutrient. About 50 per cent of people will require more and about 50 per cent of people will require less than the EAR. The LRNI is the lowest level of nutrients that might provide an adequate intake for most people. Food labels sometimes include guideline daily amounts (GDAs), which show the average amount of fat, calories, saturated fat, carbohydrate, total sugars, protein, fibre, salt and sodium to be eaten each day for adults.

The Scientific Advisory Committee on Nutrition (SACN) has now replaced COMA. They are currently in the process of reviewing the UK's nutritional requirements through the Energy Requirements Working Group.

Carbohydrate

Carbohydrates are a group of substances found in both plants and animals. Most of the carbohydrate in our diet comes from plant sources. Carbohydrates can be divided into sugars and non-sugars. Non-sugars include starch and **NSP** (non-starch polysaccharide), also known as dietary fibre. Since the early 1980s, nutritionists have recognized the importance of non-sugar carbohydrates and have promoted these as a major source of energy and nutrients.

Protein

The word protein comes from the Greek word meaning 'holding first place'. Proteins are essential in the structure and function of all living things; without them no life can exist. There are millions of different proteins – plant, animal and human – but all are built from the same units. These units are called **amino acids**. Plants combine nitrogen from the soil and air with carbon and other substances to produce amino acids. These are then built into proteins by plants. Humans either obtain their proteins by eating plants, or by eating animals that have first eaten plants.

Fats

All living cells contain some fat in their structure because **fatty acids** are an essential part of cell walls. Plants manufacture fats through photosynthesis (a process also used by plants to make carbohydrates). Animals use or store the fat they eat. If excess carbohydrate or protein foods are eaten these are also stored in the body as fat. Current dietary advice encourages us to reduce our intake of some fats and increase others.

Vitamins and minerals

Vitamins and minerals are known as micronutrients because they are essential in small quantities to ensure good health. Vitamins are organic substances, which means they come from living material or substances that were once living. Minerals are non-organic compounds that come mainly from the soil. Examples of minerals are calcium, iron and phosphorus.

Flour power

Wheat flour

All types of flour have been processed from cereals or grains. Cereals and grains are the seeds of cultivated grasses and include wheat, rye, oats, barley, corn and rice. Most of the flour used in the UK comes from wheat. There are a variety of wheat flours made from different types and different parts of the wheat grain.

Classifying wheat

Wheat can be classified as either 'winter' or 'spring'. Winter wheat is grown in the UK, Australia, Canada, Russia and the USA. It is known as hard wheat because it is high in the proteins glutenin and gliadin. Spring wheat is called soft wheat and is low in protein. It is grown in the UK and southern USA.

Milling flour

Milling is the process of changing grains of wheat into flour. It is carried out at a flourmill either by stone grinding or roller grinding. The grains are first cleaned and then conditioned by either adding or removing moisture. The bran (outer layer of grain) is separated from the endosperm (inner part of grain that is mainly starch). The amount removed depends on the type of flour being produced. The particles are then ground into granules.

Types of flour	Ideal uses
White flour: produced from hard and soft wheats to give an all-purpose flour. Self-raising varieties have a raising agent added to them in controlled, evenly distributed proportions.	Plain: pastries, batters, sauces, fruit cakes, some biscuits Self-raising: cakes, some biscuits, scones
Sponge flour: produced from soft wheats to achieve a low protein, fine flour, with an added raising agent. It can absorb more moisture than normal self-raising flour.	Cakes and sponges
Strong white flour: produced from hard wheat so it has a high protein content.	Bread, pizza bases, rolls, some scones, puff pastry
Wholemeal flour: contains the whole grain. High bran content can result in 'heavy' products as the bran interferes with gluten development. Self-raising varieties of wholemeal flour are available.	Plain: bread, biscuits, fruit cakes, some pastries, pizza bases, sauces Self-raising: cakes, biscuits, scones
Granary malted brown flour: mixture of strong plain brown flour and grains of malted wheat; high in protein.	Bread, pizza bases, rolls, some scones and teabreads

Nutritional value

The nutritional value of flour depends on the type, but all flour provides starch. Wholemeal (also called wholegrain) and wheatmeal flours are also high in **NSP**, which is important in the prevention of constipation and other bowel disorders. Since 1956 all white flour produced in Britain has been fortified with the B vitamins, thiamin and nicotinic acid, as well as the minerals iron and calcium. This is to compensate for their loss during the extraction process of milling. It is a legal requirement for calcium carbonate to be added to all flours, except wholemeal, to improve the calcium intake in the British diet. Chemicals, known as improvers, can be added in very small amounts to improve baking quality. They include potassium bromate, chlorine dioxide, azodicarbonamide and ascorbic acid.

Working properties

Flour is a carbohydrate food because it contains a high proportion of starch. Structurally, flour is a **polysaccharide** consisting of large molecules, so it is insoluble in water. Starchy foods are made more appetizing through processing and cooking. Processing disrupts the starch granules, making them easier to digest.

Gluten: The strong flour used to make bread contains two proteins: glutenin and gliadin.

 Flour is used in many different products.

When mixed with water these proteins form another protein called **gluten**. Gluten is essential in bread-making because it allows the dough to stretch and become elastic.

A network of gluten is developed during the kneading of dough. When baked, the gluten enables the dough to stretch as bubbles of gas are produced by the yeast. Once the dough has risen sufficiently, the gluten **coagulates**. This produces a loaf with a good volume and open texture.

Gelatinization: If flour is shaken or stirred with cold water it does not dissolve. However, if the mixture is heated (for example, when making a sauce) the liquid **diffuses** into the granules, causing them to swell and thicken the mixture. This thickening process begins at 60°C and is known as **gelatinization**. If the resulting 'sol' is left to cool, the mixture thickens to become a 'gel' (imagine leftover sauce that has gone cold).

Dextrinization: Many flour products become a golden brown colour when cooked, for example toast and pastry lids. This is due to the dextrin in starch, which forms brown-coloured compounds called pyrodextrins when flour products are heated.

Extraction rates

The extraction rate of a flour is the percentage of whole wheatgrain remaining in the flour after milling:

Wholemeal flour	100%
Brown flour (wheatmeal)	85–90%
White flour	70–72%

Not just chips

Staple potato

Although potatoes are vegetables they are being considered separately because of their versatility and widespread use in Western diets. Potatoes have traditionally been regarded as a **staple** food in the UK and they are still frequently eaten as part of a main meal. However, the variety of potato products available today means that not everybody automatically associates what they are eating with the humble potato! For example, potatoes are used in the production of microchips, croquettes, fritters, alphabet potatoes, waffles, wedges and fish cakes.

Nutritional value

Potatoes contain starch, which means they are classified as a carbohydrate food. Although they are not especially high in vitamin C, if eaten on a regular basis they can contribute to a person's vitamin C intake. Potatoes provide small amounts of protein, iron, potassium, B vitamins and folate (folic acid). However, the nutritional value of potatoes alters significantly depending on the way in which they are prepared. For example, boiled potatoes provide 0 g of fat per 100 g, whereas fried chips provide 9 g of fat per 100 g (which gives chips a calorific value three times higher). Also, a boiled potato that has been peeled provides 1.5 g of **NSP** per 100 g but the same amount of jacket potato supplies 2.7 g of NSP. So, when aiming for a healthy, varied diet it is important to think about cooking methods as well as the food being eaten.

Cooking potatoes

While numerous processed potato products are available in shops, there are also a variety of ways in which potatoes can be prepared at home. They can be mashed to a creamy consistency either with a splash of milk or, to make a rich version, with cream, butter or cheese. Flavourings can be added such as herbs, garlic or pesto. Alternatively, potatoes (particularly small, new potatoes) can simply be boiled, preferably with their skins on, and then sprinkled with parsley before serving. For something a bit different, potatoes can be sliced and laid in a dish with onion rings and milk, then baked in the oven. Large potatoes can be cut into thick chunks and baked until crisp and golden brown.

The main reason why potatoes are so versatile is because they come in many different varieties. Certain varieties suit particular cooking methods. Basically,

These meals all include potatoes in one form or another.

Variety	Description	Possible uses
King Edward	White skin with some pink colour; cream to pale yellow flesh; floury texture	Baking, chipping, roasting, mashing
Kerr's Pink	Pale skin; cream flesh; floury texture	Roasting, mashing
Maris Piper	Cream skin; cream flesh; floury texture	Boiling, baking, chipping, roasting
Nadine	Cream skin; cream flesh; firm, waxy texture	Boiling, roasting
Charlotte	Pale yellow skin; yellow flesh; waxy texture	Boiling, salads

potatoes can be classified as having waxy or floury textures. Waxy potatoes keep their shape well during cooking whereas floury potatoes (as the name suggests) break up and soften quite easily when cooked.

The chart above lists some potato varieties and their suggested uses.

Fat chips

The bigger the chip the better! Weight for weight, large chips contain less fat than thin ones. If this doesn't make sense, weigh 100g of French fries and 100g of chunky chips. Count the number of chips in each portion. The French fries will contain more chips. If all those fries were flattened out you would see that they have a greater surface area than the fat chips. The larger the surface area, the more fat is absorbed during cooking (and eating). So, if you've got a choice, choose fat chips!

Some chips are healthier than others.

Storing potatoes

Potatoes should be stored in a cool, dry place that is well ventilated. Air needs to be able to circulate around the potatoes so they should be removed from any packaging.

Grains of rice

Rice is the grain of a cultivated grass and is believed to be native to India and Indo-China. There are about 7,000 varieties of rice but they can be put into two general categories:

Long grain rice: four to five times greater in length than width; grains remain separate when cooked; for example, Basmati.

Short grain rice: Short, plump grains that tend to remain moist and cling together when cooked; for example, Arborio.

Although rice can be amber, it tends to only be classed as brown or white. Brown rice contains bran so as well as providing more **NSP** than white rice, it is also slightly higher in protein, iron, calcium and vitamin B. However, brown rice does require a longer cooking time.

When is rice not rice?

Wild rice is actually the seeds from wild aquatic (water) grass rather than a grain. The seeds are long, slim and black in colour.

Multicultural rice

It is estimated that over half the world's population depends on rice as a major part of its diet. It is a **staple** food in many areas, including India, China and Japan, although each favours a particular type of rice and method of cooking. Indian **pilaus** require a dry rice, while Japanese and Chinese dishes need a short-grain that is easy to shape with the fingers and can be held using chopsticks. The Italian arborio rice makes a creamy risotto, while short-grain pudding rice is ideal for sweet milk desserts.

Nutritional values

After harvesting, rice grains go through a milling process that 'polishes' the rice to remove the husk and, for white rice, the bran. Removal of the bran also removes most of the B vitamins. The deficiency disease beriberi has been a problem in the Far East where rice is highly polished and the thiamin (vitamin B1) is lost. This disease is easily overcome with the introduction of vitamin B1 into the diet. However, the main nutrient supplied by rice is carbohydrate, in the form of starch, as well as a small amount of protein and calcium. Traditionally, rice has been eaten as a natural remedy for digestive disorders as the body can break it down and absorb it easily.

Processing rice

Grains of rice can be processed beyond milling to produce rice flour, flaked rice and ground rice. These ingredients are used in puddings, cakes, biscuits and as a thickening agent for soups or stews. Rice can also be 'puffed' during the manufacture of puffed rice cereals and rice-cake snacks. Alcoholic drinks such as Japanese sake are made with rice. This wine is served warm in conical cups.

It is now possible to buy 'quick-cook' or 'easy-cook' rice for which the cooking time has been greatly reduced. The product has been partly cooked, causing the starch to **gelatinize**. It is then dried under special conditions, causing a slight expansion of the internal structure. The end result has a sponge-like texture, which absorbs water quickly and easily.

 Rice is grown in paddy fields in India.

Working properties

As starch is the energy store of plants, it is not surprising that rice (along with other plants such as cereals, root vegetables and potatoes) contains starch. Starch is made up of two **polysaccharides**: amylose and amylopectin. Different plants contain different amounts of these compounds, but the higher the amount of amylose, the easier it is for the starch in that plant to 'gel'.

When rice is cooked in water the starch granules swell as water is absorbed and so the grains soften. During this process of gelatinization, the starch molecules spill into the liquid. If rice is overcooked it becomes very gelatinous. The water used for cooking rice is often whitish in colour due to the release of starch. If rice is used as part of a meal, for example in a risotto, it helps to thicken the dish, and rice flour and ground rice are sometimes used as thickening agents.

Benefits of rice

During the digestion and absorption of rice, starch is broken down to release glucose, which can be used for energy when required. It is considered healthier to obtain energy from rice because it is a 'slow-release' carbohydrate, rather than sugar, which provides 'instant' energy. As rice does not contain **gluten** it is suitable for **coeliacs** who must follow a gluten-free diet.

Plant	% of amylose content (by weight)
Rice	16
Sweet potato	18–20
Potato	20–23
Wheat	22–25

Perfect pasta

Simply pasta

Like all foods that are a good source of complex carbohydrates, or **NSP**, (such as rice, potatoes and oats), pasta is not high in fat or calories. However, the addition of rich ingredients such as cheese, butter and cream can make a pasta dish fattening. Unfortunately, many of the delicious foods traditionally associated with pasta meals do contain a lot of fat, but there are also plenty of healthier options. For example, sauces packed with tomatoes, peppers and onions provide lots of flavour in addition to the vitamins and minerals they supply. Pasta can be the foundation for numerous simple, healthy meals that are quick to prepare.

What is pasta?

Pasta, which literally means 'dough', is traditionally a **staple** food of Italy, although it is now popular throughout the Western world. Pasta can be divided into two categories: fresh and dry. Fresh pasta is made with flour and eggs and was traditionally made at home, while dry pasta is factory-made using a flour and water paste. The flour chosen for pasta-making comes from durum wheat, which produces fine, gritty particles of amber-coloured semolina flour. The prepared pasta dough is cut, pressed and moulded into a variety of shapes, sizes and designs, some examples of which are shown in the photograph. Fresh pasta has become quite popular with today's consumer and can be bought from chill cabinets. However, for the pasta to have an extended shelf-life it has to be pasteurized and so has had some pre-cooking.

As well as the familiar whitish pasta, a brown wholewheat version is also available which obviously provides more NSP. Additional ingredients can contribute different colours and flavours, for example eggs make a yellow pasta with a rich flavour; spinach produces green pasta; and tomato provides a red colouring. Rather unusually (and at a price), black pasta is made by adding squid ink to the dough. Herbs trapped between paper-thin layers of homemade pasta have a delicately decorative effect.

Pasta can be bought fresh or dried.

The stripes in this ravioli are created using spinach and salmon.

Shaping up

There is a huge variety of pasta shapes available today and each type has its own name. However, trying to learn all the names can be difficult because in Italy the name and shape varies from province to province. There are no hard and fast rules governing which type of pasta should be used for which dish, but clearly some lend themselves to certain dishes more than others. For example, sheets of lasagne are often used to sandwich layers of meat and béchamel sauce. Cannelloni and rigatoni can be stuffed and baked in the oven, whereas ravioli and tortellini are ready-filled parcels to be served with a sauce. If pasta is boiled, it should be in lots of water so that the pasta has enough space to move about, and it should be stirred occasionally to prevent it from sticking together.

Athletic pasta

Anyone who is serious about their fitness and health must ensure that they are eating an appropriate diet. About 60 per cent of all daily calories/kilojoules come from foods high in complex carbohydrates, which includes pasta. This is because carbohydrate food is stored in the muscles and is readily converted to energy when it is needed. During digestion,

carbohydrate foods are eventually broken down into the **monosaccharides** glucose and fructose. Once these monosaccharides reach the liver (via the bloodstream) even the fructose is converted into glucose.

Any glucose that is not immediately required by the body is then stored in the muscles and liver in the form of glycogen. Glycogen is made up of many glucose units joined together. Glycogen can be converted back to glucose when the body requires energy. It acts as a reserve of carbohydrate for the body. During exercise the body prefers to use glycogen as fuel rather than blood glucose. However, if exercising for a long period of time (over an hour) the body starts to use blood glucose as glycogen stores become depleted. If exercise continues, blood glucose levels will need to be topped up with regular glucose drinks. If the muscles and liver have sufficient glycogen stores, the excess glucose is converted by the liver into fat and stored in the body.

Nutritional value of white, boiled spaghetti (per 100 g)

Energy	104 kcal/435 KJ
Protein	3.6 g
Starch	21.7 g
Sugars	0.5 g
Fat	0.7 g
NSP	1.2 g
Niacin	1.2 mg
Folate	4 mg
Calcium	7 mg

Satisfying cereals

Cereal grains

Cereals provide an important source of carbohydrate in the diet. Rice and wheat have already been mentioned but other cereals include rye, oats, corn and barley. In addition, many products are made from cereals such as couscous, polenta, semolina and cracked wheat.

Rye

Rye is a cereal grain that can grow in a cold, arid climate. Although it is similar to wheat in composition, its **gluten** lacks elasticity, so rye bread tends to be quite dense with a low volume. Crispbread is a popular rye product and rye is also used in the manufacture of some drinks including American whisky, Russian beer and Dutch gin.

Oats

Oats are both versatile and extremely good for you. They can be used to make a hearty breakfast such as porridge or are added to muesli products. Like all starchy foods, the starch in oats **gelatinizes** when heated with a liquid, and so causes porridge to thicken during cooking. Oats can be left to soak in a liquid to soften them, making them easier to digest. Oats and oatmeal can be added to cakes and cookies, while bread rolls are sometimes given a rustic look with a sprinkling of oats on top. Jumbo oats are a larger version of the porridge oat and can be used in the same way.

Although some oats contain about 7 per cent fat, which is more then most other cereals, they are an excellent source of soluble **NSP** or

Cereals are important because they provide healthy energy.

dietary fibre. NSP can be divided into soluble and insoluble forms. Sources of soluble fibre are believed to reduce the levels of **cholesterol** in the blood, whereas insoluble fibre helps to reduce the risk of constipation and other bowel disorders by assisting the passage of waste matter through the digestive system.

Corn

Also known as maize, corn is a **staple** food in Mexico and is used to make many American food products such as cornbread. Other products made using corn include cornflour, cornmeal, popcorn, cornflakes, corn syrup and corn oil. Due to its high starch content, cornflour is often used as a thickener in the preparation and processing of food products.

Barley

Barley is a staple food of the Middle East. In the Western world it is used mainly in the form of malt by brewers and distillers. Pearl barley is a product of barley that is sometimes added to stews and soups. It is high in carbohydrate so it has good thickening properties. However, it contributes little in the way of vitamins.

Breakfast cereals

A number of breakfast cereals are made by modifying or processing cereals in some way. Very often these cereals are fortified with various nutrients such as B vitamins and iron. However, depending on the type, they can also be high in fat and sugar and low in NSP.

Shredded wheat is made from whole wheat. It is cooked under pressure with water to gelatinize the starch. The soft grains are shredded to produce thin strands, which are then folded into layers to form 'biscuits'. Finally, the edges are crimped and the biscuits are dried in ovens.

Puffed cereals are made using barley, corn, rye, wheat and rice. To make puffed wheat, the grains are put in a puffing gun where the pressure is increased with the addition of steam. After cooking, the pressure is suddenly released causing a rapid expansion of the water vapour inside the grains. The end result is an expanded grain with a soft, honeycomb texture.

Cereal products

Semolina: made up of yellow, coarse particles that come from the endosperm (inner part of the grain) of wheat. It is used to make pasta dough.

Couscous: finely ground semolina is mixed with water and flour to make the little 'pellets' of couscous. It is cooked very quickly either in water or by steaming. It originates in North America and is an excellent alternative to rice. Couscous is also the name of a spicy Moroccan dish, consisting of a stew on a bed of couscous.

Polenta: also called cornmeal; it can be made into a type of porridge or used to make cornbread.

Cracked wheat: also known as bulgur (or burghul); this is processed wheat and is popular in the eastern Mediterranean and Middle East. It can be baked, cooked as a **pilau** or soaked and served raw in a Lebanese salad called tabbouleh.

Sweet as sugar

Simple sugars

The structure of all carbohydrates is based on a common saccharide unit (a simple sugar). Carbohydrates can contain from one to many thousands of saccharide units and they can be classified as shown below:

> sugars:
> **monosaccharides** (one unit)
> disaccharides (two units)
>
> non-sugars:
> **polysaccharides** (many units)

There are three types of monosaccharide: glucose, fructose and galactose. The disaccharides (which consist of two monosaccharides linked together) are:

- *sucrose* – chemical combination of glucose and fructose units, also known as table sugar; occurs naturally in cane sugar and sugar beet and in some roots (such as carrots) and fruits
- *maltose* (*malt sugar*) – chemical combination of two glucose units; formed when starch is broken down during digestion; used in the production of beer

- *lactose* (*milk sugar*) – chemical combination of glucose and galactose; occurs only in milk, including human milk; less sweet than sucrose or glucose.

Inside, outside

Sugars can be divided into intrinsic and extrinsic categories, as shown below:

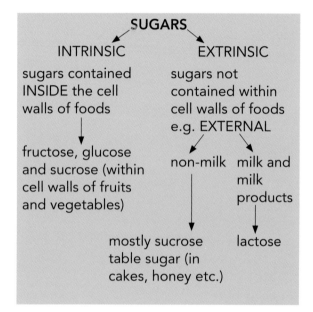

SUGARS

INTRINSIC — sugars contained INSIDE the cell walls of foods → fructose, glucose and sucrose (within cell walls of fruits and vegetables)

EXTRINSIC — sugars not contained within cell walls of foods e.g. EXTERNAL → non-milk → mostly sucrose table sugar (in cakes, honey etc.) / milk and milk products → lactose

Sucrose

Sucrose is the ordinary sugar used to sweeten food and drinks. It is also naturally present in some fruits and vegetables. Sugar cane and sugar beet contain relatively large amounts so it is from these plants that sugar is extracted commercially.

Sugar cane and sugar beet both contain about 15 per cent sucrose. Cane is grown in tropical countries and the sugar is extracted by

This man is harvesting sugar cane in Bolivia.

crushing the canes and spraying them with water so the sugar **diffuses** out. The sugary solution is treated with lime and carbon dioxide (CO_2) to remove impurities. The raw sugar is then separated from the **molasses** by **centrifugal** spinning. The raw sugar now contains about 96 per cent sucrose. Refining is needed to crystallize the sucrose, which involves further centrifuging, washing, and more treatment with lime, CO_2 and charcoal. Next, vacuum evaporation removes water under reduced pressure using 'vacuum pans', which ensures there is no discoloration. The sugar crystals are then spun in centrifugal separators to remove the syrup. Finally, the sugar is air dried.

Sugar beet is grown in more temperate climates such as the UK. The beets are sliced and steeped in hot water to extract the sucrose. After purification with lime and CO_2 the solution is evaporated and crystallized. Once again the crystals are separated from the remaining syrup and molasses by centrifugal force, and then dried.

Molasses is used by animal feed producers and food manufacturers. It can also be fermented to produce rum. The remaining syrup is used to make golden syrup or soft brown sugar.

Working properties

Sugar can contribute to the preparation of food products in a variety of ways. It:

- acts as a sweetener and is often added to processed savoury foods to make them more appealing to consumers (for example, tomato sauce);
- improves colour either by adding brown sugar or through non-**enzymic** browning (the Maillard reaction), which occurs during baking if carbohydrate and protein exist in the same product (for example, in cakes). The reaction between carbohydrate and protein molecules causes a golden brown colour to occur;
- helps baked products stay moist and extends their shelf-life because it is hygroscopic (absorbs water easily);
- can be beaten with fat so the sugar crystals separate and break up the fat, allowing more air to be incorporated;
- prevents the development of **gluten**, ensuring products have a soft and tender texture after baking;
- delays **coagulation** during baking due to its high boiling point, so sweet products can rise fully before they set;
- acts as a preservative in the production of jams and jellies. A high concentration of sugar means there is insufficient moisture for bacteria to survive;
- makes food look more attractive.

Sugar plays an important role in the successful production of sweet products.

Sweet treats

Types of sugar

There are many different types of sugar and
most are produced with specific purposes
in mind.

White sugars	Coloured sugars	Syrups
Caster: fine crystals; used for baking, confectionery, desserts and for sprinkling over food.	Barbados: dark brown, moist; small crystals of refined white sugar treated with dark-grade molasses.	Maple: best known as an accompaniment to pancakes and waffles; also used in items such as maple butter, maple sugar cake, cookies and ice cream.
Cube/loaf: refined and crystallized sugar that has been moistened and compressed into squares or rectangles; also available in brown; often used in drinks.	Soft light brown: small crystals of refined white sugar treated with light-coloured molasses.	Corn: made from maize (corn) by converting the starch to glucose syrup; used for a variety of manufactured products including drinks, canned fruits and baby foods.
Granulated: refined sugar with large granules; used for general purpose cooking; often referred to as 'table sugar'.	Demerara: refined white sugar treated with light-coloured molasses and no added colour; used in baking.	Golden: specially processed to obtain a golden colour; hydrolysed to reduce water content; stabilized to prevent fermentation in the can; used in baking, with pancakes, etc.
Icing: powdered sugar that contains anti-caking agent to prevent lumps forming; it is used in baking and as decorative topping; also available unrefined.	Coffee: similar to granulated but darker in colour, with larger crystals that dissolve slowly in coffee.	Fruit: made from white sugar, water, and fruit such as rose hip or blackcurrant; used as a base for drinks, ice cream toppings and desserts.
Preserving: large crystals; used to help eliminate the scum that forms during the making of preserves such as jam.	Rainbow: crystals of various colours; coloured using vegetable dye; used for decorative purposes.	Treacle: blend of refinery syrups and molasses; dark coloured with strong flavour; used in desserts and cakes.

Sugar confectionery

Sugar confectionery, more commonly called 'sweets', includes boiled sweets, toffee, caramel, fillings for chocolates, marshmallows, fudge and nougat. Different types of sweets can be produced by:

- adding fat or milk to the mixture
- adding flavouring agents
- altering the water content
- altering the temperature/cooking time.

When a concentrated solution of sugar (a syrup) is heated, the temperature at which it will boil depends on the amount of water present in the solution. The longer a solution is allowed to boil, the more concentrated the solution will become because as the water evaporates the boiling point of the mixture rises. Soft sweets, such as fudge, require lower cooking temperatures than hard sweets such as butterscotch.

Many sweets have a characteristic caramel flavour, produced by the caramelization that occurs when some of the sugar molecules break down during heating. As the surface of the sugar is heated to above its melting point (about 175°C) it changes to an amber colour. A good example of this is the crunchy topping on a crème brulée.

Sugar and teeth

If sugar and sugary foods are eaten on a regular basis the concentration of sugar can damage the teeth. Sugar provides the right condition for bacteria to multiply in the mouth, resulting in the production of acid. These acidic conditions cause tooth enamel to demineralize (break up). Saliva can restore the mouth to a normal **pH** about thirty minutes after the sugar has been eaten.

Hello honey

Honey was used as a sweetener long before sugar. As far back as the 10th century brewers used it to make a fermented drink called mead, and honey was frequently used in the baking of bread. Honey is a natural product, made by bees, although it can now be made artificially, using dextrose, flavourings and colourings. Bees collect the nectar from flowers and break it down with their saliva. The resulting honeycomb structures in the bees' hives are uncapped by machine and the honey is extracted using **centrifugal** force. The honey is then pumped into a strainer, filtered and packed.

The flavour and colour of natural honey is determined by the variety of flower chosen by the bees. As there are many species of flower, there are also many varieties of honey (over 200 in the United States, for example). Honey is used both as a spread and in the production of cakes, biscuits and desserts.

 There is a wide variety of types of sugar and honey.

Pure milk

Mother's milk

Humans, like all other mammals, produce milk to nourish their young. However, unlike other mammals, humans continue to consume milk after weaning (the introduction of solid food into a baby's diet) but the milk they have comes from other animals.

Human milk provides a complete diet for a baby during the first few weeks or months of life. It contains sufficient nutrients for the baby to survive until its energy demands cannot be met by milk alone. Although human milk lacks iron, a baby is born with sufficient stores of this mineral to keep it supplied until it starts to eat solid foods. If a mother cannot or chooses not to breast-feed, powdered milk can be used instead. This is cows' milk that has been specially processed to make it suitable for human babies. One advantage of breast-feeding is that **antibodies** can be passed from mother to baby, providing a certain amount of immunity to diseases.

Milk's structure

Although most of the milk consumed in the UK is from cows, other animals supply milk too, such as goats and sheep. The chart below compares some values of a range of milks:

Animal	% fat	% protein	% lactose
human	2.0–6.0	0.7–2.0	6.0–7.5
cow	3.8	3.3	4.7
goat	4.2	3.7	4.5
sheep	5.3	6.3	4.6

Milk contains three major proteins: casein, lactalbumin and lactoglobulin. Casein is found in milk and milk products only and accounts for about 78 per cent of their total protein content. Milk is a high-quality protein as it contains all the essential **amino acids** (those that cannot be made by the body). Practically all the minerals present in soil, and therefore grass, are present in milk. These include calcium, phosphorus, potassium, magnesium, sodium, chlorine, sulphur, iron, zinc, silicon, copper and fluorine. Milk is a particularly good source of calcium and phosphorus, which are essential for skeletal growth.

Milk is also a good source of vitamins A, B1 and B2. Vitamin D is present in milk fat. However, the amount varies depending on the time of year because cows exposed to sunlight produce milk with a higher vitamin D content. A small amount of vitamin C is present in fresh milk.

Milky emulsions

Milk exists in the form of a natural emulsion which means it has globules of fat floating in it. As milk is an oil-in-water emulsion, it has more liquid than fat. If ordinary pasteurized milk is left to stand, the fat will float to the top because fat is lighter than water. However, during homogenization milk is forced through tiny holes under pressure, causing the fat globules to break up and remain suspended throughout. This is why cream does not float to the top of homogenized milk.

Types of milk

Almost all milk sold in the UK has been pasteurized. Green top or unpasteurized milk can be sold from farms holding a special

Milk is used in the production of numerous products including cheese, yoghurt, cream, ice cream, buttermilk and smetana (a cultured product like a thin, sour cream).

licence but pasteurization kills about 99 per cent of spoilage organisms and so reduces the risk of food poisoning. Other heat treatments include sterilization and ultra heat treatment (UHT), which both involve higher temperatures and longer cooking times, and result in milks with a longer shelf-life. Evaporated milk has been sterilized and then reduced through evaporation, making it thicker and more concentrated. Condensed milk is evaporated and sugar is added to produce a very sweet, thick substance. Milk with different fat contents (skimmed, semi-skimmed and whole milk) are usually available.

Boiling over

When milk is heated the proteins **coagulate**. This can be seen when milk is heated in a saucepan. As the temperature rises, a skin of protein forms on the surface, trapping steam below. If heating continues, the milk will boil over and spill. During prolonged cooking the lactose (milk sugar) caramelizes, creating a distinct flavour that is associated with sterilized and UHT milks.

If milk is mixed with an acid ingredient, the **pH** falls, causing the protein casein to coagulate. This is known as curdled milk and may be a desired effect, for example when rennin (an **enzyme**) is added during the production of cheese or when lactose is changed into lactic acid by bacteria during the souring of milk to make yoghurt. However, curdling is not always desired, for example when making custard with eggs, the mixture will look like scrambled (curdled) eggs if it is allowed to get too hot.

Meat matters

Muscular meat

'Meat' is the flesh of an animal that is eaten as food. This is usually muscle, connective tissue and fat. Meat is different from offal and poultry although these, too, come from animals. Offal is liver, kidneys, heart and brains. Poultry includes chicken, turkey, duck and goose. However, the flesh of an animal cannot necessarily be used as meat as soon as the animal is dead. A number of chemical changes occur before the product has the right colour, texture, flavour and ability to cook. For example, following slaughter the muscles of an animal will experience *rigor mortis* which means they stiffen and set. Eventually, the muscles soften again and then the animal is left to 'age' to allow various **enzymic** processes to occur.

Meat is a good source of protein as well as B vitamins and iron, and it provides all the essential **amino acids** needed by the body for growth and repair. Offal also supplies vitamins A and D. Different types and cuts of meat provide differing amounts of fat, but animal fat is predominantly **saturated**. Concern about fat in the diet has led to a decline in the consumption of red meat in recent years, with a corresponding rise in the sale of chicken.

Muscle structure

Muscle tissue consists of roughly three-quarters water and one quarter protein. The animal muscle that converts to meat is called striated muscle and consists of long muscle fibres that run parallel to each other. Muscle fibres are held in bundles by connective tissue and usually the smaller the bundles, the more tender the meat. Individual muscle fibres are divided into myofibrils surrounded by fluid. The myofibrils contain two types of protein: myosin (thicker filaments) and actin (thinner filaments). These proteins are responsible for the contracting of muscles. The harder muscles work when an animal is alive, the tougher the meat will be prior to cooking.

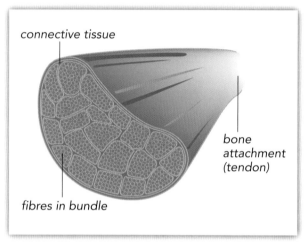

connective tissue

bone attachment (tendon)

fibres in bundle

 This is a cross-section of muscle tissue.

Making connections

Connective tissue contains two proteins: collagen and elastin. Collagen forms the main connective tissue within and around muscles and is the main component of tendons. Collagen is white in colour and flexible, but not as elastic as elastin. Collagen forms **gelatin** when cooked. Elastin is yellow in colour and does not convert to gelatin. It forms the main component of ligaments that attach bones or cartilage.

Fat is found in the connective tissue of muscles. This is called *invisible* fat and is often referred to as 'marbling'. A certain amount of marbling is desirable in meat as it helps to keep the meat moist. *Visible* fat is easily identified by its creamy white-yellow colour. The yellowness is due to the pigment carotene (chemically related to retinol or vitamin A). Older animals and those eating carotene-rich foods produce meat with a yellower fat. The fat stored under the animal's skin is known as subcutaneous fat.

Cooking meat

Meat is cooked to make it safe to eat by destroying harmful bacteria. Cooking also improves its texture, colour and flavour. Meat that is difficult to cut or hard to chew is said to be 'tough'. It has longer, thicker muscle fibres and more connective tissue than tender meat. However, it is possible to improve the tenderness of meat through mincing it or pounding it with a meat hammer. **Marinades** that contain acidic ingredients, such as wine, also help to tenderize meat. Tough cuts of meat tend to be cooked using long, slow methods such as stewing, while tender pieces can be cooked quickly as in grilling.

Colour changes

The colour of meat is mainly due to the pigment myoglobin. This pigment accounts for about 75 per cent of the total pigment of red meat. Some muscles contain more of this pigment than others; for example, chicken legs are darker than breast meat due to the myoglobin content. The degree of pigmentation is related to muscle use (well-used muscles and those from older animals are darker). Colour changes in meat during its preparation and cooking are as follows:

	CUT	HEAT
myoglobin	oxymyoglobin	haemochrome
	⟶ bright red	⟶ greyish/brown

This meat is on display in the butcher's section of a supermarket.

Pricey protein

Although meat is still an important source of protein in the UK, protein can be produced more quickly and cheaply by other means. Lean beef contains only 25 per cent protein, whereas low-fat soya flour contains 50 per cent protein. The decline in the sale of red meat over the last decade may be as a result of some of the following issues:

- the high cost of meat
- an increased concern for animal welfare
- an increase in vegetarianism
- health concerns such as coronary heart disease
- the BSE scare.

Fishy stuff

Fish as food

There are many hundreds of fish species used as food. These fish can be categorized as follows:

Demersal fish are found at the bottom of the sea and include 'round' fish, such as cod and haddock, and 'flat' fish, such as plaice and sole.

Pelagic fish are found at mid-depth and near the surface of the sea. They tend to be fatty fish such as mackerel and herring.

Freshwater fish include salmon, trout, carp, perch and pike.

Shellfish are divided into crustaceans (for example, shrimp, crab and prawns) and molluscs (for example, mussels, cockles and oysters).

Fish is a highly perishable food because it deteriorates rapidly. Most fish are packed in ice or frozen immediately after they are caught, and remain that way until sold. The reduced temperature helps to arrest the bacterial growth that leads to decay. The unpleasant smell associated with 'off' fish is due to a nitrogen-containing compound in the flesh, which is broken down by bacteria if the fish is stored incorrectly or for too long.

Buying fish

When choosing fresh fish from a fishmonger or supermarket, the fish should smell pleasant – like the sea, rather than 'fishy'. If eyes are present they should be bright and not sunken. The skin must be firm, shiny and moist. Smoked fish should smell fresh but with a

 Fish and shellfish are packed in ice in order to slow down the growth of bacteria.

smoky aroma and the flesh should look glossy. Fresh and smoked fish are best stored separately to avoid a transference of aromas. Frozen fish must not have any sign of thawing or damage and should be frozen throughout. Fish should be stored in the fridge (below 5°C) or freezer (−18°C). It is best to cook fresh fish on the day of purchase as it has a short shelf-life.

Fish structure

The structure of fish is similar to meat in that they both possess bundles of short muscle fibres held together by connective tissue. However, the connective tissue of fish is very thin and only contains collagen, with no tough elastin. This is why fish is easier and quicker to cook than meat. Fish muscles are arranged into 'flakes', which are usually clearly visible in cooked fish.

The nutritional value of fish varies according to its type. Obviously the fat content of oily fish is much higher than that of white fish. The fat in white fish is stored in the liver (hence the name of cod liver oil). The fat in oily fish is distributed throughout its flesh but, as in white fish, the fat is **polyunsaturated**, unlike that found in meat.

All fish is a good source of high biological value protein (it contains all the essential **amino acids** in the right proportion). However, as it has a higher water content than meat, it provides less protein than the same weight of meat. There is no carbohydrate to be found in fish but it can easily be combined with foods high in carbohydrate, such as fish and chips or fish pie. Fish can be a good source of the minerals calcium and phosphorus, especially if the bones are eaten (as in canned fish) and

sea fish offers plenty of iodine. Potassium and sodium are also present in all fish. Oily fish are excellent sources of the fat-soluble vitamins A and D, and B vitamins are present in fish in small amounts.

Cooking fish

Fish requires only a short cooking time and moderate temperatures because its muscle fibres are short and there is little connective tissue. The collagen in the connective tissue dissolves easily and is then converted into soluble **gelatin**. Fish is cooked sufficiently when its protein has **coagulated** – this process begins at about 60°C. To test whether fish is cooked, part the flesh gently to see if it falls into 'flakes'. Once cooked, white fish becomes less opaque and shellfish changes from grey or brown to pink in colour. Unlike meat, fish is usually cooked in small portions and so it is easily overcooked, making the flesh rubbery and tough.

Fatty fish

It may seem like a contradiction to all other 'healthy' messages but fatty fish is definitely believed to be good news! This is mainly due to the type of fat it contains. Oily fish such as mackerel, tuna, salmon, sardines, trout, pilchards and herrings possess **fatty acids**, which encourage the liver to produce HDL (high-density lipoprotein). HDL is also known as 'good' cholesterol because it helps to eliminate 'bad' cholesterol (LDL) from the body. LDL is the type that is deposited in blood vessels and contributes to the risk of a heart attack, angina or stroke. A diet that contains oily fish can also reduce the symptoms of arthritis, such as inflammation and painful joints.

Eggs

Convenience food

Eggs may be regarded as the ultimate convenience food. With very little excess packaging and waste, they can form the basis of a very easy but nutritious meal in minutes. Just think about some of the uses for this versatile product:

- eggs on their own – scrambled, boiled, fried, hard-boiled, omelette and poached
- eggs as an ingredient – pancakes, cakes, biscuits, scones, breads, pastries, quiches, flans, egg curry, egg sandwiches, egg custard, egg salad, soufflés, ice cream, mousses.

Highly nutritious

Eggs are an excellent and relatively cheap source of protein. They contain all the essential **amino acids** required by humans. Eggs also provide the fat-soluble vitamins A and D as well as B vitamins and the minerals zinc and iron. Eggs have been associated with raised blood **cholesterol** levels, but in fact the type of cholesterol they contain is broken down by the body and excreted.

Smart egg

Today some eggs are enriched with Omega 3 fatty acids by feeding hens a diet of oil-rich seeds. This transforms eggs into **smart foods**.

Structure

A hen's egg weighs about 60 grams and its main parts are the shell, white and yolk. The egg white makes up about 60 per cent of the total weight. Thick and thin regions make up the white. The yolk, in the centre of the egg, is held in place by strands of protein known as the chalaza. The degree of yellow depends on the hen's food and any colourings added to the feed.

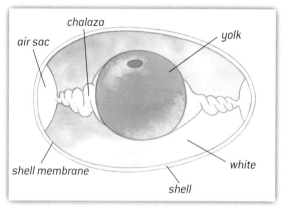

 Structure of a hen's egg.

The delicate but tough outer shell is made from calcium carbonate (chalk) and its colour is determined by the breed of hen that laid it. The shell is porous so that air can pass through, allowing the chick to breathe and moisture to evaporate. Inside the shell there are two very thin membranes (designed to protect the chick if the shell gets cracked). These layers separate the shell from the white. A newly laid egg will have a tiny pocket of air at the wide end. As time passes and more air gets in, so the air pocket grows. Moisture is also lost from the egg and the membrane inside the shell becomes loose as air continually passes through it.

Working properties

Eggs can perform a whole array of functions in food preparation and cooking.

Emulsions: An emulsion is a mixture of a fatty substance and a watery substance. These do not stay mixed together naturally, which is why they need the help of an **emulsifier**. Egg yolk contains lecithin, which is a natural emulsifier and is used in the manufacture of many food products such as cakes. It works because one part of its molecule is hydrophilic (loves water) and the other part of its molecule is hydrophobic (hates water). The molecules of lecithin surround the droplets of, for example, oil so the hydrophilic part of the molecule is in the water and the hydrophobic part is in the oil. That is how the mixture is kept smooth and uniform.

Foam formation: A foam is actually very small bubbles of gas (often air) dispersed throughout a liquid. Foams are often used in food preparation, for example in making swiss rolls, meringues and mousses. When egg whites are whisked, bubbles of air are surrounded by albumen (egg white protein) that has been stretched and dried in the whisking. This elasticity is essential so that when the foam is baked, the incorporated air can expand without breaking the cell walls and before the ovalbumin is **coagulated** by the heat of the oven. However, overbeating means too much air has been incorporated and the protein becomes thin and less elastic.

Coagulation: The coagulation of egg protein is responsible for the thickening effect that eggs have in products such as custards. Egg white begins to thicken as the temperature reaches 60°C, and at 65°C it will no longer flow. At 70°C the white is fairly firm. The coagulation of egg yolk begins at about 65°C. Coagulation only occurs over a period of time, although it occurs more rapidly as the temperature increases. Examples of products that rely on egg protein coagulation include traditional stirred custards, baked custards, quiche Lorraine, flans, cakes and poached and boiled eggs.

 Eggs are incredibly versatile and can be used in the production of a wide range of products.

Soya beans

Soy or soya?

Soya beans are small, oval beans that have been used in oriental diets for many years. They grow on the soya bean plant and are used in the production of soya bean curd (also called tofu), soya bean flour, textured vegetable protein, soy sauce, soya milk, soya oil and the Japanese sauce, miso. The beans grow in a range of colours (yellow, green, red and black) and are high in nutrients, especially protein. The names 'soy' and 'soya' refer to the same products.

Soya products are a better source of protein than many other plant proteins (before fortification, or the addition of nutrients) because they contain all the essential **amino acids**. Soya is also rich in potassium and supplies useful amounts of magnesium, phosphorus, iron and folate. It contains small amounts of the mineral manganese and vitamins B6, B1 and vitamin E.

Tofu

Tofu is made by grinding cooked soya beans to produce a milk. This is then **coagulated** with the addition of calcium sulphate. The result is a creamy coloured soft cheese-like product that is high in protein, low in fat and free from

 These soya products are all good sources of protein.

cholesterol. Although tofu itself is bland, it readily absorbs other flavours. This means that it works well with **marinades** and spicy foods. Tofu is used in oriental dishes and as a meat substitute for vegetarians and vegans.

Textured vegetable protein

Soya beans are used in the production of a high-protein vegetarian product called textured vegetable protein, or TVP. The beans are pressed to extract their oil, then ground into a flour. The resultant fat-free soya flour is mixed with flavourings, colourings and water to produce a dough. After heating, the dough is 'extruded' or forced through a nozzle. On hitting the air at the other end of the nozzle, the dough expands into a spongy, textured mass, which is then dried. The final step is to shape it into chunks, flakes or granules that can be used in vegetarian products or added to meat dishes to 'extend' the more expensive meat protein. Foods that have been developed to resemble meat are called 'meat analogues' and these are part of a group of foods known as **smart foods**.

Soya oil and flour

Soya oil and flour are processed and used either on their own or in manufactured products. For example, soya flour is sometimes added to bread to make it whiter and soya oil is used in some margarine and cooking fats.

Soy sauce

Soy sauce often appears in Chinese and Japanese recipes. It is used in small amounts as a condiment (seasoning) in dishes. It is made by fermenting soya beans to produce a dark, concentrated liquid.

Soya milk

Soya milk, an extract of the soya bean, is used by vegetarians, vegans and those allergic to cows' milk and/or lactose. Lactose is the sugar (carbohydrate) present in milk. Soya milk is also used in various non-dairy drinks that may also contain a natural sweetener and flavouring. These may be fortified with vitamins and minerals and are often produced using organic farming methods.

Like all beans, soya beans can be sprouted for their shoots. Fresh beansprouts should look ivory white with a slight yellow on their tips. They are an excellent source of vitamin C and can be eaten raw or cooked. They are often used in oriental dishes such as salads, soups, pancake rolls and stir fries.

Help or hinder?

Soya contains plant oestrogens called phytoestrogens. They have a similar structure chemically to the oestrogens in our body. It has been suggested that these phytoestrogens can help protect against some cancers and **osteoporosis** and may reduce symptoms during a woman's **menopause**. A comparison is often made between the Japanese and European diet and the incidence of coronary heart disease as evidence of the benefits of soya. However, more recent reports have questioned the health benefits of soya. The amount of soya eaten in the UK and other European countries remains well below that consumed in Japan and China, where soya has been a part of the diet for many years and with no reported ill-effects.

Pulsating pulses

Edible seeds

Plants from the legume family produce seeds, called pulses, which can be purchased fresh or dried. These include peas, beans and lentils and they have been a **staple** food in many parts of the world for thousands of years. Mexico, for example, first cultivated kidney, pinto and black beans, while lima beans were traditionally eaten in Peru. Broad beans and chick peas came from the Middle East. China is famous for soya beans and adzuki beans, while Africa developed dishes using black-eyed peas and pigeon peas. Today, pulses are available worldwide and their use has increased with the growing interest in meat alternatives.

Peas

Chick peas look like creamy coloured hazelnuts and, when cooked, have a nutty flavour. They are extremely versatile and can be milled into flour, roasted whole or ground after cooking. They are the main ingredient of the Middle Eastern dish, hummus, which is a savoury dip. Dried peas were a popular vegetable before the introduction of frozen peas, although 'marrowfat' peas with their tough skins and soft texture are still eaten, too.

Beans

The only pulses available in a supermarket twenty years ago would probably have been butter beans, haricot beans, split peas and red lentils. Nowadays, there is generally a wide choice to set your pulse racing. Butter beans are a versatile vegetable because they can be eaten cooked, alone or in casseroles and stews, or eaten cold in salads. Believe it or not, baked beans start life as haricot beans, which are a creamy colour and can be bought without the tomato sauce, either dried or in a can. Red kidney beans became popular in the UK through the Mexican dish, chilli, and some canned kidney beans are now labelled 'chilli beans'.

Adzuki beans originated in the Far East. They are small, dark red or black beans with a sweet flavour. The Italian borlotti beans have a speckled skin and are used in casseroles and salads. Mung beans are also known by their Indian name, moong dal. They are small, green

These dishes are all made with pulses.

beans that are widely used in China where they are sprouted for their shoots. Less well known here are pigeon peas, a staple food in the Caribbean. They are small, round, beige beans with a sweetish flavour. Other beans include flageolet, cannellini, pinto, lima and black-eyed beans.

Lentils

Lentils are usually identified by their colour, which can be orange, brown, grey, yellow, green or black. They look like round peas but their size varies and they may be sold split or whole. Lentils tend to be associated with Indian cookery because they form the main ingredient of dahl (or dal), which is a main or side dish served with curry. Cooked lentils form a soft purée so they work well in soups and, unlike other pulses, they do not usually require soaking before cooking.

Drying out

In order to produce dried peas, beans or lentils, the legumes must be dried as quickly as possible after harvesting so there is no loss of flavour, plumpness or texture. Many dried pulses can be bought cooked and canned to reduce preparation time. Dried pulses can be stored for six to nine months after purchase as long as they are kept cool and dry.

Cooking beans

One advantage in cooking with pulses is that they readily absorb other flavours. For example, when preparing a bean salad, it is best to pour over the dressing while the beans are still hot because the warm starch contained in the beans will absorb the oil like a sponge, improving both the flavour and texture of the salad. Some pulses become soft and mushy on heating so the appropriate bean should be chosen for each dish (although in some cases one pulse can be successfully substituted for another).

 Pulses are high in protein and provide dishes with an interesting texture.

Most dried pulses need to be soaked before cooking in order to make them edible, and cooking times can be quite long, depending on the variety. Red kidney beans can actually cause food poisoning if they are not sufficiently boiled prior to cooking. It is recommended that any required salt should be added after pulses have been cooked otherwise they become hard and unpalatable. All pulses are high in protein but if they are served with a cereal food, 30 per cent more protein will be available to the body due to the combination of **amino acids** present in both foods. Many traditional pulse dishes include a cereal, such as rice or bread, as an accompaniment, beans on toast being a good example.

Animal fats

Fatty acids

Animal fats such as butter and lard are solid at room temperature and, like all fats, are greasy in texture. All fat molecules contain carbon, oxygen and hydrogen atoms that are linked in a specific and unique way. The most important fats in nutrition are **triglycerides** and these are made up of one molecule of glycerol and three **fatty acids**.

Usually, three different fatty acids are attached to the glycerol molecule so a huge range of fats is available. Fats do not consist of a single type of triglyceride. For example, in butter the main fatty acids attached to glycerol are butyric, oleic and stearic acids, but there are 69 different fatty acids actually present.

Physical character

The type of fatty acid present within a triglyceride will determine its physical characteristics. A triglyceride made up mainly of short-chain fatty acids is likely to be a hard fat and one consisting mainly of long-chain fatty acids could be liquid at room temperature. The hardness of a fat also depends on the proportion of **saturated** and unsaturated fatty acids present.

Plastic fat

Solid fats gradually melt over a range of temperatures rather than at one fixed temperature. This can be seen when melting butter in a saucepan – the butter slowly melts on the outside while the centre remains intact. This ability to remain soft over a range of temperatures is known as plasticity. The plasticity of a fat is due to it being a mixture of different triglycerides, each one having its own melting point.

Butter

Butter is a natural product made by churning cream. It can be purchased salted, unsalted or slightly salted and, by law, must contain at least 80 per cent fat and no more than 16 per cent water. Butter supplies vitamins A and D, although the amount varies according to the time of year. Summer butter has higher values because the cows are outside eating grass and are exposed to the sun. The colour is also affected due to higher levels of carotene (a plant pigment). Butter contains saturated fatty acids although, because butter is produced naturally, many people now believe that it is better to eat butter in moderation rather than to eat manufactured margarine.

 Butter can be creamed with caster sugar to make cakes.

Lard

Lard is almost 100 per cent fat and is produced from pig's fat. It is a white, solid fat with a bland flavour and is high in saturated fatty acids. However, some 'healthier' versions are now available for cooking.

Fatty functions

Butter is the traditional fat associated with cake-making. Cakes rely on the incorporation of air into the fat during production and butter has the ability to hold tiny bubbles of air when it is beaten. Although this process is much easier if butter is at room temperature, the use of food processors take the hard work out of 'creaming' cakes. The addition of caster sugar helps the aeration process. Butter also adds a characteristic colour and flavour to many food products, from cakes to sauces.

Lard does not have good aeration properties and its bland flavour and poor colour makes it a less popular choice for cakes, biscuits or sauces.

The solidity of lard and butter at room temperature makes them useful in the preparation of products such as shortbread and pastries. A 'short' or crumbly texture can be achieved by 'rubbing-in' the fat to the flour. Each flour particle is then coated with a water-proof layer of fat, preventing any liquid in the recipe from coming into contact with the proteins in the flour. If **gluten** (a protein) is allowed to develop, the result would be tough and chewy. Lard is particularly good as a 'shortening agent' although if used with butter (as in traditional shortcrust pastry) there is the added value of colour and flavour.

Butter and lard are not usually recommended for frying as they have a low **smoke point**, which means they will decompose easily, causing an unpleasant flavour and odour. Animal fats also deteriorate quite rapidly due to oxidative rancidity. This is the process of the spoilage of fats which result in 'rancid' fats. Oxidative rancidity is caused by a reaction between the unsaturated fats and oxygen, so fats should always be covered and stored in the fridge below 5°C.

 Fat is rubbed into flour as part of the first stage of making pastry.

Vegetable oils

Liquid lipids

Fats and oils are collectively known as lipids. Oils are a mixture of **triglycerides**, just like solid fats, but they contain a high proportion of triglycerides with a low melting point so are liquid at room temperature. Most vegetable oils are liquid at 20°C, although coconut oil and palm oil are two exceptions. Unlike their solid partners, oils have a relatively high proportion of mono- and **polyunsaturated fatty acids**.

Vegetable oils are usually extracted from seeds, kernels or nuts and are used in deep or shallow frying, in salad dressings, sauces or **marinades**, and also to brush over foods.

How refined?

Oils can be divided into two categories: refined and unrefined. Refined oils are produced using modern methods in which the fruit, seed or grain is cleaned, crushed and heated at the same time as pressure is applied. The oil produced is then filtered to remove any solid particles. Some refined oils are chemically treated to extend their shelf-life; these tend to sell for lower prices.

Unrefined oils are produced using a more complicated method. Their higher price is due to the fact that, for example, five kilograms of olives are needed to produce just one litre of unrefined virgin olive oil. To make unrefined olive oil, the fruit is crushed between grinding mills and the pulp is then pressed while the olives are cold (known as cold pressing). The oil is channelled out and left to settle in a dark place with a controlled temperature.

Olive oil

Olive oil has been popular with the Greeks for many years – they are now thought to consume 25 litres per person every year! You may well have noticed all the different types of olive oil in the shops, as well as the corresponding variation in price. This is due to its fatty acid content. If the oil contains more than 3 per cent oleic acid it is labelled 'pure olive oil' or simply olive oil. However, if it contains less than 1 per cent it is called 'extra virgin' olive oil.

Olive oil has been promoted by health experts due to its high proportion of unsaturated fatty acids. A recent study, reported in the *Journal of Epidemiology and Public Health*, found that olive oil offers more protection against bowel cancer than fruit and vegetables.

Vegetable oils

There are a number of different types of vegetable oil:
- Sunflower oil is a popular oil used for shallow frying and in salad dressings. It is useful to blend sunflower oil with a more expensive oil to save money. It should not be confused with safflower oil, which is more golden in colour.
- Corn oil is another inexpensive oil with a high **smoke point** and so can be safely used for frying.
- Rapeseed oil has the lowest saturated content of all the oils and has been used in the Mediterranean and the East for many years.
- Soya bean oil is used in the production of margarine and can be used in salad dressings.

A variety of oils are available for consumers to buy.

Seed oils

Sesame seed oil, a brown oil made from toasted sesame seeds, is popular in China. It is also available as a lighter oil with a delicate flavour. Mustard seed oil is made from both brown and black mustard seeds and tends to be used in preserves and for cooking. It is common in India and is sometimes used to replace ghee, the clarified butter used in Indian cooking.

Nut oils

Groundnut or peanut oil has a high smoke point, so is suitable for frying. It can also be used to make mayonnaise or vinaigrette. Walnut oil is an expensive, richly flavoured oil produced by pressing new or green (unripe) walnuts. However, it does deteriorate quickly so it is best to buy it in small quantities. Other nut oils include macadamia, almond and hazelnut. With the exception of groundnut, nut oils burn easily and are best used in dressings.

Hydrogenation

Hydrogenation is the process of making oils more solid. Most margarines are made using hydrogenation. The process involves the addition of hydrogen to the double bonds of the unsaturated fatty acid molecules. This makes the fatty acids saturated and therefore more solid. While this process improves the versatility of oils, increasing the saturated content goes against their 'healthy' image.

Chocolate

Food of the gods

Chocolate is made from the fruit of the cacao tree. The scientific name for this tree is *theobromine cacao* and *theobromine* means the 'food of gods'. The cacao tree is indigenous to South America where the seeds (cocoa beans) were used by the Aztecs to make a drink flavoured with chilli, cinnamon, maize meal and water. Cocoa eventually reached England in the mid-1600s. Several Quaker families (Cadbury, Rowntree, Fry and Terry's) produced a nourishing drink using cocoa and milk to encourage people not to drink gin.

Chocolate production

It takes one year's crop from one cocoa tree to produce enough chocolate to make just twenty chocolate bars! Cocoa beans undergo a great deal of processing before the chocolate is produced. The flesh of the cocoa fruit is removed to reveal the beans which are then piled onto palm leaves where they are left in the sun to ferment. The beans are left to dry on racks and turned occasionally until they darken. They are shovelled into sacks and pesticides are applied (unless the product is organic) before being inspected. Then they can be exported.

Chocolate manufacturers have to roast cocoa beans to develop their flavour and to loosen the kernel from the outer shell. The kernels are ground and heated causing the fat to melt, leaving the cocoa mass behind. The bitter-tasting fat is called chocolate liquor. Cocoa butter is then separated from the cocoa mass using hydraulic pressure. The resulting solid cake of cocoa is ground and sifted to produce

Cocoa beans are used during the production of chocolate.

cocoa powder. Chocolate is made from chocolate liquor and cocoa butter. Although chocolate varies, it is generally made with the addition of sugar, milk (for milk chocolate) and vanilla extract. A natural **emulsifier** called lecithin may be added, too.

Cocoa butter

Cocoa butter is the fat that gives chocolate its characteristic texture and ability to melt-in-the-mouth. At normal temperature, cocoa butter is solid but at body temperature it melts very quickly. However, it is this property of cocoa butter that allows chocolate to be moulded and shaped and used as a coating for sweets, biscuits and cakes.

Today the **European Union** (EU) allows up to 5 per cent of chocolate's fat to be one of five alternatives to cocoa butter. However, in the United States, the Food and Drug Administration does not allow a product to be called 'chocolate' if the fat content contains anything other than cocoa butter.

Working properties

To obtain a professional glossy finish to confectionery or to achieve a particularly chocolatey-tasting cake, it is best to use chocolate containing a high proportion of cocoa solids, often called couverture.

When melting chocolate it is best broken into small pieces first. Melting should be done using a bain-marie or double saucepan so the chocolate can melt gradually without coming into direct contact with the heat source. Chocolate burns easily because it has a relatively low melting point (113–131°C). Chocolate can be melted in a microwave if it is done carefully, using a low setting.

A process known as tempering makes melted chocolate easier to use. This involves melting some couverture chocolate to about 113°C. The cocoa butter may now be visible as white streaks in the chocolate – it is this effect that tempering aims to control. About two-thirds of the chocolate is poured onto a marble slab or smooth work-surface and spread out quickly with a flexible knife. It is drawn together in the centre and the spreading is repeated until all the streaks have disappeared. This chocolate is returned to the original bowl and mixed.

Carob

An alternative to chocolate comes from the carob plant – its pods produce a mild version of cocoa. Carob does not contain stimulants but when made into chocolate it is just as high in fat and calories!

 Eating chocolate cake can give you that 'feel-good' factor.

Feel-good factor

Chocolate is associated with feeling good and it is often eaten as a reward or to cheer yourself up. This is because chocolate is believed to boost serotonin and endorphin levels in the brain, which are responsible for making us feel 'uplifted'. However, chocolate contains the stimulants theobromine and caffeine, which increase alertness and add to chocolate's addictive nature. In fact, one 125 gram bar of dark chocolate contains more caffeine than a cup of instant coffee! Chocolate supplies some protein and potassium, and plain chocolate contains iron and magnesium, but fat is its main drawback. Chocolate is high in fat (about 30 per cent by weight) and contains varying amounts of sugar.

Fresh fruit

Categories of fruit

It is currently recommended that we should all eat at least five portions of fruit and vegetables every day. This advice is due to the vitamin and mineral content as well as the **NSP** they provide. There is a huge array of both fruit and vegetables available, which makes this nutritional advice easier to follow. Fruit can be classified as shown:

- *Berry fruits* include soft fruit such as strawberries, raspberries, blackcurrants, grapes, cranberries and loganberries.
- *Citrus fruits* are made up of juicy segments surrounded by a tough peel or skin. Some contain seeds but others are seedless. They include grapefruits, oranges, limes, lemons and kumquats.
- *Fleshy fruits* have a firm texture and may or may not contain seeds. These include melons, apples, bananas, figs, kiwifruit, passion fruit, pears, pineapples, papaya and pomegranates.
- *Stone fruits* contain just one central stone, which is surrounded by flesh. Examples are apricots, avocados, cherries, plums, peaches, mangoes, lychees and dates.

Fruity structure

Most of the edible part of fruit (and vegetables) consists of cells called parenchyma cells. Cellulose is the main component of the cell walls, which contain cytoplasm. Cytoplasm is a jelly-like substance that can move within the cell. Cytoplasm holds the nucleus, mitochondria and plastids. About 90 per cent of the parenchyma cell consists of sac-like spaces called vacuoles that contain cell sap. This watery substance is partly responsible for the juicy texture of many fruits. The cells are divided by air spaces causing some fruits, such as apples, to float on water.

All fruits soften when they are cooked due to the loss of the watery cell sap. This can easily be illustrated by comparing the crunch of a raw pear with the squidgy texture of cooked pears.

Going brown

Fruit will naturally turn brown as it ages but the process speeds up if the fruit is peeled, cut, bruised or bitten. This discolouration is the result of **enzymes** reacting with a **substrate** (such as phenolic compounds), both present in the fruit, in the presence of oxygen. The reaction is known as enzymic browning and is clearly seen in bananas, apples, avocados and pears when they are exposed to the air. The process is minimized through cooking, the addition of sulphur dioxide, by excluding air or by adding an acid such as lemon juice.

vacuole containing cell sap   cell wall   intercellular air spaces

cytoplasm

mitochondria (produce the cell's chemical energy)   nucleus (central part of cell)   plastids (storage areas)

Parenchyma cells are present in the edible part of fruit and vegetables.

The wide variety of fresh fruit available should encourage us all to include them in our diet.

Nutritional values

The nutritional value of fruit varies according to the type and whether it has been processed. Fresh fruit has a low energy value due to its high water content and low fat content. Exceptions to this include avocados and olives. Most of the carbohydrate present in fruit is in the form of intrinsic sugar (see page 16) although bananas are high in starch. Vitamin C is found in most citrus fruits, as well as blackcurrants, blueberries and kiwifruits, while vitamin E is present in mangoes and avocados; both these vitamins are antioxidants.

Super foods

It has long been known that vitamins and minerals are essential for optimum health and a lack of these can lead to diseases such as **scurvy** and **rickets**. Research shows that some vitamins and minerals can also protect our health. Micronutrients, known as antioxidants, help our bodies fight the damaging effects of free radicals. Certain fruits (as well as other foods) have been labelled 'super foods' due to their concentration of usable nutrients. Super foods include blueberries, pomegranates, avocado, strawberries, tomatoes, and even goji berries from China!

What are free radicals?

Oxygen is needed by our bodies to convert food into energy. This process results in by-products called free radicals. Free radicals are unstable and reactive molecules. They are also produced as a result of stress, exposure to too much ultraviolet light from the sun and environmental pollutants such as cigarette smoke and car exhaust fumes. Free radicals destroy the body's cells and damaged cells result in injury to body tissue. This may take the form of heart disease, certain cancers (especially stomach, colon, breast and lung), arthritis, cataracts and Parkinson's disease. Free radicals are also thought to be a major factor in ageing and the formation of skin wrinkles. Not all free radicals are harmful. We need some for our immune system to fight infection and also for some enzymes in the body. Trouble arises when too many form in our body.

Various vegetables

Vegetable categories

Vegetables can be grouped according to where in the ground they grow. Those that grow beneath the soil include roots, bulbs and tubers, while stems, leaves, flowers and fruits or seeds can be seen growing on or above ground level. Examples from each group are listed below:

- Roots – carrots, parsnips, swede, turnip, radish, kohlrabi, salsify, beetroot
- Bulbs – leeks, onions, shallots, spring onions
- Tubers – potatoes, sweet potatoes, yams, Jerusalem artichokes
- Stems – celery, fennel, asparagus
- Leaves – Brussels sprouts, all types of cabbage, all types of lettuce, Chinese leaves, chicory, spinach, mustard and cress, curly kale, spring greens, watercress
- Flowers – broccoli, cauliflower
- Fruits and seeds – globe artichokes, okra, all types of bean, courgettes, cucumber, peas, marrows, aubergines, peppers, plantains, pumpkins, sweetcorn, tomatoes, all types of mushrooms.

Nutritional value

Like fruit, vegetables have a high water content and low energy value. Very small amounts of protein are present in vegetables;

 Frozen vegetables are convenient and often retain their vitamins.

those vegetables with the most are the pulses. They are all low in fat. Some varieties contain the carbohydrate starch, such as potatoes, while others are higher in intrinsic sugar (another form of carbohydrate). All vegetables provide useful amounts of **NSP** although the actual amount will depend whether the skin is eaten.

Spinach and watercress offer significant amounts of calcium, while iron is supplied by spinach, broccoli and frozen peas. Carotene (chemically related to retinol or vitamin A) is present in orangey coloured vegetables such as carrots and tomatoes. The antioxidant (see page 39) vitamin E is found in significant amounts in spinach, watercress and broccoli, while another antioxidant, vitamin C, is present in green peppers, Brussels sprouts and broccoli. In addition, the B vitamins including folate (folic acid) are found in small quantities in most vegetables.

Vitamins

Some vitamins such as vitamin C (also called ascorbic acid) and the B group, are water soluble. This means that if they are soaked or cooked in a lot of water they can **leach out** of the food and into the liquid. Unless the liquid is to be eaten as part of the meal (as in a casserole), the vitamins will be lost. Vitamin C is also readily oxidized, which means when vegetables (or fruit) containing it are exposed to air, the vitamin will be destroyed. However, there are strategies that can be used to help reduce the risk of destroying vitamins in vegetables:
- choice – only choose fresh vegetables with no bruises or blemishes
- storage – use immediately if possible; if not, store in a cool, dark place
- preparation – prepare just before using; remove dirt but do not soak; use a sharp knife and only cut as much as necessary; tear leaves of green vegetables rather than cut; the addition of lemon juice to exposed surfaces can reduce vitamin C loss
- cooking – use a minimum of water; add vegetables to the water when it is boiling; cook quickly; microwaving and steaming are excellent for vitamin retention; serve and eat immediately.

Frozen vegetables are very good nutritionally. This is because they are frozen very quickly after harvesting, which retains most of their nutritional value. When buying fresh vegetables there is a danger that they have been hanging around in storage for weeks, by which time the vitamin and mineral content will have diminished.

Cooking vegetables

The structure of vegetables is very similar to that of fruit. During the cooking of vegetables the cell membranes are broken down causing a loss of water from the cells. This is the reason why water-soluble vitamins are lost into cooking water. Also, the intercellular gas (air spaces) is replaced by water, making the vegetables translucent and soft. This results in a loss of volume as seen during the cooking of spinach, which wilts within seconds.

Vegetable colour

The colour of green vegetables is due to the pigments chlorophyll a and b. The pigments are fat soluble and found in the plastids of the cell (see page 38). The green colour can be enhanced with the addition of bicarbonate of soda, which makes the cooking water less acidic. However, this is not advisable because it also destroys the vitamin C.

Salty sodium

Excessively salty

The first thing to note about salt is that we generally eat far more than our bodies need. In fact, we probably eat twice the recommended six grams a day. The government has set the Food Standards Agency a target to reduce the salt intake of the population to 6 grams per person per day by 2010.

Full of flavour

The main reason why salt is added to food is to enhance the flavour. Salt is often said to 'bring out the flavour', thereby making our eating experience all the more pleasurable. However, we also have a need for the inclusion of salt in our diet. Salt (sodium chloride) is necessary to maintain an internal water balance within the body. Salt is easily absorbed and any excess is removed by the kidneys and excreted in urine. Some is also lost through sweating. When sodium is removed from the body, water is lost as well and this is why we become thirsty after eating salty food. Too much salt in the diet can lead to fluid retention, resulting in swollen limbs which can be both unsightly and uncomfortable. This condition, known as oedema, may cause increased weight.

Potassium

In addition to sodium chloride, our bodies also require the mineral potassium. Both sodium and potassium are involved in the transmission of nerve impulses and in muscle contraction, including the beating of the heart. The body is very careful to balance the body's content of these two minerals, so if salt levels are high then potassium will be low, but if potassium levels are high, then the salt level will be minimal. Anyone who feels their salt intake is high would do well to increase their intake of potassium-rich foods such as bananas, tomatoes, dried fruits and fresh fruit juice, in order to counterbalance the sodium levels.

Processed foods

The high salt intake amongst many people today is largely due to the consumption of processed foods. Many types of processing have an adverse effect on the flavour of foods, so salt may be added to boost flavours. Always check the labels on foods such as soups, sandwiches, pasta sauces and ready meals, so you can choose those with less added salt.

Of course, salt will be listed in the ingredients on food products, so its presence should be obvious. However, monosodium glutamate (MSG), the flavour enhancer, may also be listed and consumers should be aware that this is a high sodium product.

 Processed foods tend to be high in salt.

Reading labels

As well as looking at the ingredients list on food labels, the amount of salt in a product may be found on nutritional charts. In this case, it will say 'sodium' because it is the sodium part of sodium chloride that we should eat less of. Excessive concentrations of sodium in the body can lead to high blood pressure, some stress and nervous symptoms and possibly even to kidney disease. High blood pressure is also a risk factor in coronary heart disease and stroke.

If a food label lists 0.3 grams sodium per serving, then this figure needs to be multiplied by 2.5 to work out the sodium chloride (salt) content. So, if 0.3 grams of sodium are consumed, this amounts to 0.75 grams of salt. (Remember, the recommended amount per day is 6 grams.)

Using salt

Sodium chloride has traditionally been used as a means of preserving meat and fish, a process known as curing. Examples of cured meat available today are bacon, ham and salami. Salt is also used to help produce the

Types of salt

Rock salt – occurs naturally in strata; formed by evaporation of brine

Sea salt – from the sea; filtered, heated and artificially evaporated

Pretzel salt – flat flakes; mined in the Gulf of Mexico

Block salt – refined rock salt

Bay salt – from evaporated sea water

crunchy crackling on pork and, due to salt's absorbency, it is sometimes sprinkled over raw, sliced aubergines to bring out the bitter liquids they can contain.

Substituting salt

Anyone suffering from high blood pressure will almost certainly be advised to avoid salt in their diet. Some people prefer to use a salt substitute rather than cut it out altogether. These are usually based on potassium but it may be wise in the long run to train the palette to enjoy less salty foods.

 Salt comes in many forms but it is best not to consume too much of it.

Resources

Books

Dictionary of Food Science and Nutrition
(A & C Black, 2006)

GCSE D&T Food Technology: Complete Revision and Practice, Richard Parsons
(Coordination Group Publications, 2005)

GCSE Design and Technology for AQA: Food Technology Student Book, Lesley Woods
(Heinemann Educational Publishers, 2005)

Making Healthy Food Choices (series)
(Heinemann Library, 2006)

Oxford Dictionary of Food and Nutrition (2nd edition), David A. Bender
(Oxford University Press, 2005)

The Cook's Bible of Ingredients, Margaret Brooker (New Holland Publishers, 2005)

Websites

www.britegg.co.uk
The British Egg Information Service website provides information about egg safety, egg products, nutrition, the Lion quality mark and recipes.

www.foodstandards.gov.uk
The Government's information website for the Food Standards Agency contains details of their aims, research, committees, regulations and press releases. It also addresses topical issues such as food labelling and packaging.

www.eatwell.gov.uk
This site provides the latest news from the Government's Food Standards Agency relating to food and health. Topics include healthy diet, keeping food safe, food labels and health issues.

www.plus44.com/heritage/cheddar/cheese.html
The website of the Cheddar Gorge Cheese Company in Somerset gives details of how real cheese is made.

www.potato.org.uk
A comprehensive website providing lots of information about potatoes as well as links to other websites such as www.lovechips.co.uk, www.potatoesforschools.org.uk and www.britishpotatoes.co.uk.

www.bbc.co.uk/health/healthy_living/nutrition
This site provides lots of information about different foods, dietary requirements and the needs of people at various stages of life.

www.fabflour.co.uk
Educational material as well as information about nutrition and healthy eating in relation to bread and flour is available on this site.

www.grainchain.com
This is the education site from the Flour Advisory Bureau.

Contacts

British Nutrition Foundation
High Holborn House
52–54 High Holborn
London
WC1V 6RQ
Tel: 020 7404 6504
www.nutrition.org.uk

Institute of Food Science & Technology
5 Cambridge Court
210 Shepherd's Bush Road
London
W6 7NJ
Tel: 020 7603 6316
www.ifst.org
Gives information on food-related training and careers.

Sustain (previously The National Food Alliance)
94 White Lion Street
London
N1 9PF
Tel: 020 7837 1228
www.sustainweb.org
Publications focus on food and its production, looking at how food is grown, manufactured, transported and stored.

The Flour Advisory Bureau Ltd
21 Arlington Street
London
SW1A 1RN
Tel: 020 7493 2521
www.fabflour.co.uk
Provides resources and information about wheat and flour.

The Food & Drink Industry National Training Organisation
6 Catherine Street
London
WC2 5JJ
Tel: 020 7836 2460
www.foodanddrinknto.org.uk
More information on training and careers in food and drink manufacturing.

Places to visit

Cadbury Trebor Bassett
PO Box 12
Bournville
Birmingham
B30 2LU
Tel: 0121 458 2000
www.cadbury.co.uk
School resources are available. Cadbury's World is hands-on entertainment for children, providing an insight into the history of chocolate and current production.

Van den Bergh Foods Limited
Brooke House
Manor Royal
Crawley
West Sussex
RH10 2RQ
www.vabfoods.co.uk
Provides nutritional information and recipes using Olivio, a vegetable fat spread and Olivio olive oil.

Glossary

amino acids   proteins are made up of simpler substances called amino acids, some of which are essential in the growth and development of our bodies. Amino acid molecules join to form long chains; there are around twenty amino acids and the chains can be very long, so a huge number of proteins are available.

antibodies   proteins that are formed in the blood if an unwanted substance (disease) invades the body. Antibodies fight the substance and try to eliminate it.

centrifugal   movement away from the centre; centrifugal spinning starts in the centre and moves outwards

cholesterol   fatty substance naturally present in the body. If blood cholesterol levels become unduly high there is a danger that the cholesterol will clog up arteries, preventing the natural flow of blood.

coagulate   irreversible process in which proteins 'set' when heat is applied

coeliacs   coeliac disease is a condition that causes the wall of the small intestine to become damaged if gluten is eaten. Gluten is a protein found mainly in wheat but it is also present in rye, barley and oats.

dietitian   person who works with individuals or groups of people to help plan their diet. A dietitian may work for a hospital or private clinic. In the UK, training and state registration (legal permission to practise) is controlled by law.

diffuse   to move slowly from one place to another. For example, liquid moving into granules of starch as the mixture is heated during the making of a sauce.

emulsifier   substance that enables two other substances to remain mixed together when they would naturally separate. For example, oil and vinegar are immiscible (they do not stay mixed) but if egg yolk is added (for example, when making mayonnaise) the mixture remains combined. This is due to the natural emulsifier, lecithin, present in egg yolk.

enzyme/enzymic   protein that speeds up metabolic reactions. If an apple is cut and left exposed, the flesh will turn brown due to enzymic browning.

European Union   alliance of 27 countries who aim to work and live together cooperatively

fatty acids   organic acids that form part of the structure of fats and oils (along with glycerol). Fatty acids can be classified as saturated or unsaturated.

food technologist   person who works for a food company or manufacturer to develop and test new food products

gelatin   soluble protein prepared from collagen or animal bones; used in sweets, canned meats and jelly desserts

gelatinize   if a starch food is heated with a liquid, the liquid diffuses into the starch granules, causing them to swell and thicken the liquid

gluten   protein found in wheat that is a blend of two proteins (glutenin and gliadin). Anyone with an allergy to or intolerance of gluten (coeliac disease) is reacting to gliadin.

leach out   to move out of one substance and into another; for example, vitamins leach out of vegetables and into the cooking water when they are boiled for too long

marinade   liquid mixture used to tenderize and flavour foods (usually meat and fish)

menopause   stage in a woman's life when hormonal changes cause menstruation (periods) to gradually stop

molasses   syrupy substance remaining after sugar has been crystallized

monosaccharides   simple sugars containing one saccharide unit. When joined together, they form disaccharides and polysaccharides. All of these sugars are carbohydrates.

non-starch polysaccharide (NSP)   complex carbohydrates found in foods other than starches; also called fibre or dietary fibre. NSPs may be divided into insoluble (found in wheat, maize, rice) and soluble (found in oats, beans, rye). Vegetables and fruit usually contain both types.

osteoporosis   deterioration of the bone that occurs with age due to the loss of bone mineral and protein; often accelerated by the menopause in women

pH   measure of the amount of acidity or alkalinity on a logarithmic scale. The scale runs from 0 (strongly acidic) to 14 (strongly alkaline); 7 is neutral.

pilau   dish made from rice or bulgur; it contains vegetables, meat or fish

polysaccharide   consists of long chains of one type of monosaccharide joined together. Three polysaccharides are important in nutrition: starch, cellulose and glycogen.

polyunsaturated   fats that contain a higher proportion of polyunsaturated fatty acids than monounsaturated or saturated fatty acids. Some are essential to the efficient functioning of the body. The main source of these fats is vegetable; they tend to be soft or liquid at room temperature (for example, sunflower oil, olive oil and oily fish).

rickets   deficiency disease causing the malformation of bones in growing children; due to a deficiency of vitamin D, leading to poor absorption of calcium. Osteomalacia is the adult equivalent.

saturated fat   saturated fats have a higher proportion of saturated fatty acids than unsaturated fatty acids. Their structure means that each carbon chain has its full complement of hydrogen atoms (i.e. is saturated with them). They are mainly from animal sources and are solid at room temperature (for example, butter, lard and meat fat). A diet high in saturated fats is believed to contribute to coronary heart disease.

scurvy   deficiency disease resulting in bleeding gums and poor healing ability; if untreated it is fatal. It is caused by a lack of vitamin C and can still occur today.

smart foods   foods that have been developed through the invention of new or improved processes

smoke point   when blue smoke appears on the surface of a frying fat or oil, indicating that the fat/oil has started to decompose

staple   principal food, particularly of a country or region, and usually high in carbohydrate; for example, rice is a staple food of China

substrate   substance that allows something to happen; for example, discoloration of fruit may be caused by enzymes acting with phenolic compounds (the substrate)

triglycerides   formed through the linking of three (tri) fatty acids and glycerol

Index